I0016511

Discover Spain
Travel Journal

George Orwell once said: "I would sooner be a foreigner in Spain than in most countries. How easy it is to make friends in Spain!" That is one of the many reasons Spain is one of our favorite countries to visit. You never forget the sights, sounds, and smells (especially the aromas of pastries and baked goods) of the places you experience. I have sampled a cool glass of Sangria and slice of fresh carrot cake in Malaga, Spain and then celebrated Oktoberfest (a German celebration) with a stein of beer and a giant pretzel in the Canary Islands. Those experiences and memories are why people love travel. Over the course of many adventures, I have been fortunate to visit more than 65 countries and six continents around the world. Enjoy this travel journal and I hope you find it useful chronicling or planning your next trip. Safe travels!--Don Kojich

Photo Credits:
Front Cover: La Coruna, Spain
Back Cover: Tenerife, Canary Islands, Spain
Title: Tenerife, Canary Islands, Spain
Page 3: Las Palmas, Gran Canaria, Spain
Page 8: Cartagena, Spain
Page 13: Malaga, Spain
Page 18: Lanzarote, Canary Islands, Spain
Page 25: Malaga, Spain
Page 30: Vigo, Spain
Page 36: La Coruna, Spain
Page 41: Cadiz, Spain
Page 44: Las Palmas, Gran Canaria, Spain

"The life you have led doesn't need to be the only life you have." – Anna Quindlen

"The use of traveling is to regulate imagination with reality, and instead of thinking of how things may be, see them as they are." – Samuel Johnson

"Better to see something once than hear about it a thousand times." - Asian Proverb

"I travel a lot; I hate having my life disrupted by routine."
– Caskie Stinnett

"Two roads diverged in a wood and I – I took the one less traveled by." – Robert Frost

"The journey not the arrival matters." – T.S. Eliot

"I travel because it makes me realize how much I haven't seen, how much I'm not going to see, and how much I still need to see." - Carew Papritz

"With age, comes wisdom. With travel, comes understanding." - Sandra Lake

43

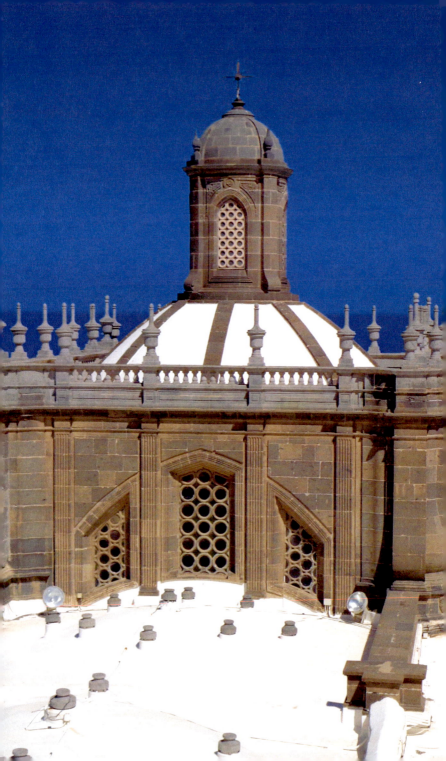

"A journey is best measured in friends, rather than miles." - Tim Cahill